OUR GREAT
AFRICAN TREASURY

MARCUS GARVEY

written by Nyere

SPINEFIRE PRESS LLC

SPINEFIRE PRESS LLC

To my beloved family.

"A people without the knowledge of their past history, origin and culture is like a tree without roots."

- Marcus Garvey

* LEADER   * ORGANIZER

* PIONEER   * LIBERATOR

* VISIONARY   * REVOLUTIONARY

Marcus Mosiah Garvey Junior

Was a courageous and charismatic Pan-African leader,

Who selflessly fought for the restoration of Black liberties,

Decades before the Civil Rights era of 1950s and sixties.

He was a firm believer in human rights, justice, and dignity,

With the view that all races are a brotherhood of humanity.

The African race was no different and certainly no less,

But its legacy was stolen and that tarnished its greatness.

To redeem the race and build a brighter future for his people,

Garvey, of his own volition, bravely led Blacks in their struggle.

He raised their consciousness, offered tools of empowerment,

So they, as Africans, could control their destiny and advancement.

He laid knowledge of self and group unity as the foundation,

As he charted the course to create a true African regeneration.

A guiding light that proved to be more than just a visionary.

His influence, his work, and his spirit were revolutionary.

Born in St. Ann's Bay on the beautiful island of Jamaica,

To his father, Malchus Garvey Sr. and his mother, Sarah,

On Wednesday, August 17th, in the year 1887.

He became their youngest child of eleven.

At birth he was named Malchus Mosiah Garvey Jr.

His father's namesake, but he changed it later.

Many called him Mosiah until he became grown,

Then the change to Marcus, by which he is known.

From an early age he began to read ravenously,

Enamored by the books found in his father's library.

A very bright learner, was always eager and keen,

But due to dire hardship he left school at fourteen.

To provide financial help to his family through its crisis,

He was sent to work in a nearby town as an apprentice.

Under the tutelage of his godfather, a very skilled printer,

He was given an opportunity to develop himself further.

"Education is the medium by which a people are prepared for the creation of their own particular civilization, and the advancement and glory of their own race."
- Marcus Garvey

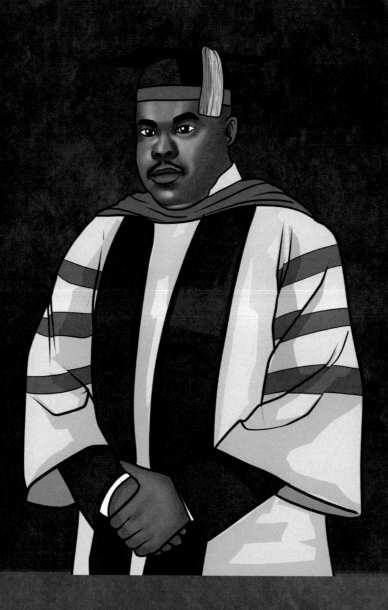

* **PAN-AFRICANIST**

* **ENTREPRENEUR**

* BLACK NATIONALIST

* **ORATOR**

* AUTHOR

* PUBLISHER

A few years later he moved to Kingston, the capital city,

To work as a compositor for the P.A. Benjamin Company.

He advanced to a master printer, then an esteemed foreman.

The first time that position was held by an Afro-Jamaican.

A very dedicated employee, but was faced with a decision,

For he was also the vice president of the printer's union.

He sided with the workers in their demands for a wage hike.

As a trusted representative he was chosen to lead their strike.

The strike failed, and he was terminated for his involvement,

But became even more encouraged to fight for fairer treatment.

Unflinchingly steadfast and resilient, he created a plan of action.

And so began *Garvey's Watchman*, his very own publication.

Living in the city exposed him to the stark racial disparity,

As well as the inequitable structure of the Jamaican society.

He saw countless Blacks negatively affected by discrimination,

Which kept many of them in poverty and a state of deprivation.

Influenced by Dr. Robert Love, a physician and Black activist,

He became more race-conscious and sought to be a catalyst.

He primed for racial justice leadership through self-education,

And worked to improve his vocabulary, writing, and elocution.

His mettle remained firm whenever faced with adversity,

Determined to turn every challenge to a new opportunity.

With confidence and purpose, he overcame each problem.

Pragmatic and disciplined in his approach to solve them.

He made his own luck as tough times befell Jamaica.

Venturous by nature, he upped and moved to Costa Rica.

There he worked as a timekeeper on a banana plantation,

A front-row view to the ruthlessness of African exploitation.

Honduras, Ecuador, every Latin American country he went,

The plight of racial discrimination was pervasive and evident.

Black workers labored endlessly building the Panama Canal.

The conditions they faced there were life-threatening and brutal.

Deeply troubled and appalled by the horrors he had to witness,

He published newspapers which highlighted the sheer injustice.

His searing editorials decried and condemned the inhumanity,

As he championed for Africans to regain their pride and dignity.

"If you haven't confidence in self, you are twice defeated in the race of life. With confidence, you have won even before you have started."
- Marcus Garvey

"Never forget that intelligence rules the world and ignorance carries the burden. Therefore, remove yourself as far away as possible from ignorance and seek as far as possible to be intelligent."
- Marcus Garvey

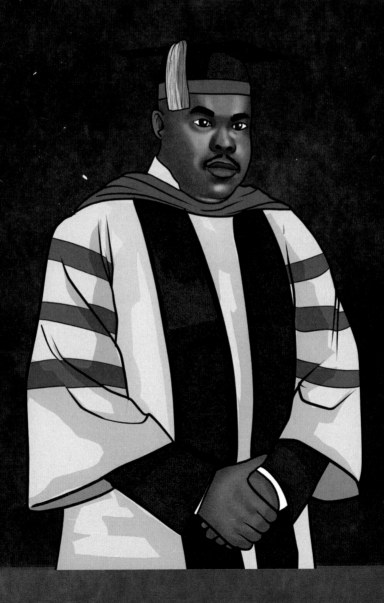

With aspirations to further his skills and knowledge,

He then traveled to England to attend Birkbeck College.

His time there was spent studying law and philosophy,

Working a few odd jobs as well as touring Europe briefly.

While working at the *African Times and Orient Review*,

A Black-owned Pan-African journal that was relatively new,

He was assigned various roles, from messenger to editor,

And used his journalistic skills as a valuable contributor.

There, intellectuals and activists wrote to advance race interests,

In which they covered a gamut of topics that raised awareness,

From Black ambitions to injustices within the British empire.

Garvey readily absorbed as much knowledge as he could acquire.

As he became enlightened, his views on colonialism sharpened.

To its far-reaching and damaging effects, his eyes were opened.

The tragic loss of land, resources, religious and cultural identity,

Crippled Africans socially, economically, and scarred their psyche.

A path to upliftment emerged as he read *Up from Slavery;*
Booker T. Washington's life-changing autobiography.
It promoted self-help, economic and social segregation,
Teaching practical skills, as done by the Tuskegee institution.

Inspired by Washington's work to encourage achievement,
His unselfish character and dedication to self-improvement,
Garvey felt energized to create something quite similar,
And filled with boundless ambition, he returned to Jamaica.

His aim was to foster unity among the Black population,
And to transform their lives by improving their condition.
He crafted plans with charity and self-reliance at the core,
And aspired to build a trade school for the nation's poor.

In July of 1914, his brainchild moved a step closer to fruition,
As he formed the Universal Negro Improvement Association.
The U.N.I.A. promoted race pride, independence, and unity,
But was met with mere disinterest towards its ideology.

* **RACIAL UNITY**

* CULTURE

* **KNOWLEDGE OF SELF**

* SOLIDARITY

* IDENTITY

* AFRICAN HISTORY

If we as a people understood the greatness from which we came we would be less likely to disrespect ourselves."
- Marcus Garvey

Not deterred, Garvey set his sights on a U.S. expansion,

And in 1916, he relocated to New York full of passion.

He settled in the district of Harlem with a strategic intent,

Armed with a vision and plans for a burgeoning movement.

From street corners to a cross-country tour,

His brilliant and rousing speeches were a huge draw.

They were poignant and clearly communicated,

And for many oppressed Blacks, they resonated.

He imparted knowledge of Africa's great history,

As the originator of art, science, and technology.

So much was brazenly taken from its great civilizations,

And used for the benefit and interest of other nations.

The African continent is the birthplace of humanity,

Steeped in history, traditions, and cultural diversity.

Africans have a rich heritage to proudly proclaim.

Their Black skin, a symbol of GREATNESS, not shame.

Among Blacks he awakened a collective consciousness,

Where pride and optimism replaced utter hopelessness.

This was the impetus for the U.N.I.A. Harlem chapter,

And the start of the influential *Negro World* newspaper.

U.N.I.A.'s message spread quickly, taking a firm grip.

Within a month it achieved two million in membership.

Worldwide, there were several million strong by 1920.

It grew into the largest Black organization in history.

Trinidad, Australia, Ghana, Panama, England, Ecuador,

Barbados, South Africa, Brazil, Cuba, and others galore.

As it expanded across the world to a multitude of nations,

The stage was set for Africans to establish better relations.

The oneness of purpose formed among African people,

Validated a kindredship that was real and undeniable.

A unified global mass in a fierce struggle for their liberty,

Organized, planned, and used their power of solidarity.

"Liberate the minds of men and ultimately you will liberate the bodies of men"
- Marcus Garvey

* MASS MOVEMENT
* NATIONALISM
* **SELF-DETERMINATION**

* **ORGANIZATION**
* **RECLAMATION**
* AUTONOMY

Within the U.N.I.A. there were various auxiliaries,

Which engaged the different generations and families.

Everyone had a role, a way to purposefully contribute.

The objective was clear, and they were wholly resolute.

The Juvenile Division served as a youth preparatory,

And the Universal African Legions was a paramilitary.

The Universal African Motor Corps ably supported them,

While the Black Cross Nurses enlisted the women.

There were international conventions, its inaugural in 1920,

When over 25,000 Garveyites convened in New York City.

They came from around the world for this month-long event,

And created, among other things, an African rights document.

A momentous time, as the Pan African flag was unveiled.

Under the red, black, and green, unity and pride prevailed.

The bond of Africans everywhere solidified in symbolism,

And raised the spirit of a people in need of nationalism.

Garvey desired for the diaspora to form its own nation,

So as to have the right to autonomy and self-determination.

For his people he envisioned them in power and prosperity,

Ultimately fulfilled through a plan for Black sovereignty.

He believed it was the surest way to achieve total liberation,

And so proposed the motherland as the place for its creation.

The rising sentiment toward Black nationalism outpoured.

"AFRICA FOR AFRICANS at home and abroad!"

To be self-ruled, with nation-building a top priority,

And to reclaim and restore a strong African identity.

The diaspora set to lay claim to its rightful place,

For Africa, by right of heritage, belongs to the African race.

A united and Black-led Africa was indeed optimal.

Liberate the entire continent and remove all things colonial.

Europeans in their Scramble for Africa stifled its development,

Which denied African people of opportunity and enrichment.

Liberia was deemed as a potential U.N.I.A. base in Africa,

For the return and settlement of those from the diaspora.

Land was to be given in exchange for U.N.I.A.'s assistance,

But those plans were later met with disfavor and resistance.

"Our success educationally, industrially is based upon the protection of a nation founded by ourselves, and the nation can be nowhere else but Africa."
- Marcus Garvey

"In a world of wolves one should go armed, and one of the most powerful defensive weapons within the reach of Negroes is the practice of race first in all parts of the world."
- Marcus Garvey

With the many plans clearly laid out for advancement,

One was to create an economy that was independent,

In which Africans invested and pooled their resources,

Owned and gave support to other Black businesses.

Garvey followed his own advice and led by example,

For he owned businesses that employed his own people.

He encouraged Africans to be land and property owners,

And furthermore, to become confident as producers.

To build for themselves what they have built for others,

With their labor, skills, talents, as creators and thinkers.

To be a strong people who are self-reliant and resourceful,

Capable to start and own businesses that are successful.

It was a means for Africans to achieve economic power,

So they as a group can rise up, stand strong, and prosper.

When organized economically to provide for their own need,

They will be self-sufficient, sustainable, and ultimately freed.

U.N.I.A.'s vision for advancement was boldly ambitious.

The support it received was encouraging and tremendous.

The membership willingly invested both time and money,

And participated in undertakings to change the trajectory.

That spirit launched the Black Star Line shipping enterprise.

Progress became a tangible reality for everyone to visualize.

A fully incorporated Black-owned and operated marvel,

That would give all Africans fair access to trade and travel.

Negro Factories Corporation spurred economic development,

Via a Black entrepreneurial economy that was independent.

It produced goods, owned a variety of shops and factories,

Sold stocks, all of which created employment opportunities.

* **MEDIA**
* EDUCATION
* RESOURCES

* GROUP COOPERATION
* **SELF-SUFFICIENT**
* INDEPENDENT ECONOMY

"You cannot depend upon another race to free you."
-Marcus Garvey

Liberty Hall, a designation given to every U.N.I.A. headquarter.

Those purposeful spaces were a requirement for each chapter.

They provided a place to have meetings, events, and activities,

Which in turn benefitted and strengthened Black communities.

Education was one of U.N.I.A.'s main ambitions,

With its goal to establish Tuskegee-like institutions.

First came Liberty University in Claremont, Virginia,

With its curricula on discipline and African culture.

Negro World was a powerful, dynamic, global newspaper.

It wielded influence and provided a space for the Black writer.

A conduit that provided pro-African messaging each week,

And garnered a circulation of over half a million at its peak.

African pride and progress rattled the colonial authorities,

Who resorted to ban the *Negro World* in many countries.

Their deep fear of Black social and economic independence,

Was becoming a reality and a grave threat to their dominance.

Among those seeking the demise of his grassroots movement,

Was the prominent and powerful United States government.

They used a broad range of tactics and laws that were unjust,

In an attempt to undermine, destabilize, quell, and erode trust.

F.B.I. agents cunningly planted spies within his entourage,

Whilst the Black Star Line was willfully crippled by sabotage.

Since Garvey broke no laws according to their investigation,

Mail fraud charges were then fabricated to get a conviction.

* PRINCIPLES

* JUSTICE

* COMMITMENT

* RESILIENCE

* LIBERATION

* UPLIFTMENT

"We are going to emancipate ourselves from mental slavery, for though others may free the body, none but ourselves can free the mind. Mind is our only ruler; sovereign."
-Marcus Garvey

He was then sentenced to five years in a federal prison.

Although his appeal failed, his spirit remained unbroken.

While incarcerated he released a few letters of reassurance,

That for the race and the cause, it was a happy sufferance.

His wrongful accusal was a grave assault on his character,

It sowed distrust and hurt the morale of many a follower.

U.N.I.A.'s membership declined, although some stayed loyal.

Overall, the association was in crisis, struggling for survival.

After thirty-three months his sentence was commuted.

Nevertheless, the president ordered that he be deported.

So, back to his homeland of Jamaica he was hastily sent,

Quite certain that his farness would pose an impediment.

The years spent in Jamaica following his deportation,

He made evident his commitment to African liberation,

And worked hard to stabilize his floundering movement,

But there was plenty of uncertainty, much to its detriment.

Despite waning influence and the challenges that were many,

He started two newspapers and even an amusement company.

His activity in politics led to a new party, which he founded,

While his involvement in social reform kept him grounded.

Years later he moved to London seeking greater influence,

Undauntedly delivering speeches to enlighten his audience.

He engaged in lecture tours, conventions, various writings,

And his School of African Philosophy for leadership trainings.

Unfortunately, he suffered a stroke in January of 1940,

Was left paralyzed, then had another one subsequently.

He died peacefully on Monday, June 10th, that same year.

One of Africa's greatest sons, though he never made it there.

"Take advantage of every opportunity;
where there is none make it for yourself."
- Marcus Garvey

"Honor black men and women who have made their distinct contributions to our racial history."
- Marcus Garvey

Marcus Garvey left behind a tremendous legacy,

As a dynamic race leader and fearless revolutionary.

His influence created many outstanding Black leaders,

Namely Nelson, Malcolm, Martin, Stokely, and others. [1]

This racial justice luminary and superbly courageous hero,

Provided guiding principles for Blacks worldwide to follow.

He believed if practiced, the whole African race will thrive.

Take time to share his story and keep his memory alive.

Safeguard African history for future generations,

Preserve stories of its people and their contributions.

The invaluable collection of the African's story,

Is **OUR GREAT AFRICAN TREASURY.**

[1] Nelson Mandela, Malcolm X, Martin Luther King Jr, Stokely Carmichael

Honorable Marcus Mosiah Garvey Jr.
(1887- 1940)

"I trust that you will so live today as to realize that you are masters of your own destiny, masters of your fate; if there is anything you want in this world, it is for you to strike out with confidence and faith in self and reach for it."

– Marcus Garvey

PAN AFRICAN FLAG

RED – the blood that unites all people of Black African ancestry, and shed for liberation.

BLACK – Black people whose existence as a nation, though not a nation-state, is affirmed by the existence of the flag.

GREEN – the abundant natural wealth and fertility of Africa.

The Indispensable Weekly
The Voice of the Awakened Negro

The Negro World

Reaching the Mass of Negroes
The Best Advertising Medium

ONE GOD, ONE AIM, ONE DESTINY

A Newspaper Devoted Solely to the Interests of the Negro Race

VOL. XX. No. 25

NEW YORK, SATURDAY, JULY 31, 1926

PRICE: FIVE CENTS IN GREATER NEW YORK
TEN CENTS ELSEWHERE IN THE U. S. A.
TEN CENTS IN FOREIGN COUNTRIES

DECLARATION OF RIGHTS OF NEGRO PEOPLES OF THE WORLD

In order to encourage our race all over the world and to stimulate it to a higher and grander destiny, we demand and insist on the following Declaration of Rights:

1. "Be it known to all men that whereas, all men are created equal and entitled to the rights of life, liberty and the pursuit of happiness, and because of this we, the duly elected representatives of the Negro peoples of the world, invoking the aid of the just and Almighty God do declare all men, women and children of our blood throughout the world free citizens, and do claim them as free citizens of Africa, the Motherland of all Negroes."

2. "That we believe in the supreme authority of our race in all things racial; that all things are created and given to men as a common possession; that there should be an equitable distribution and apportionment of all such things, and in consideration of the fact that as a race we are now deprived of those things that are morally and legally ours, we believe it right that all such things should be acquired and held by whatsoever means possible."

3. "That we believe the Negro, like any other race, should be governed by the ethics of civilization, and, therefore, should not be deprived of any of those rights or privileges common to other human beings."

4. "We declare that Negroes, wheresoever they form a community among themselves, should be given the right to elect their own representatives to represent them in legislatures, courts of law, or such institutions as may exercise control over that particular community."

5. "We assert that the Negro is entitled to even-handed justice before all courts of law and equity in whatever country he may be found, and when this is denied him on account of his race or color such denial is an insult to the race as a whole and should be resented by the entire body of Negroes."

6. "We declare it unfair and prejudicial to the rights of Negroes in communities where they exist in considerable numbers to be tried by a judge and jury composed entirely of an alien race, but in all such cases members of our race are entitled to representation on the jury."

7. "We believe that any law or practice that tends to deprive any African of his land or the privileges of free citizenship within his country is unjust and immoral, and no native should respect any such law or practice."

8. "We declare taxation without representation unjust and tyrranous, and there should be no obligation on the part of the Negro to obey the levy of a tax by any law-making body from which he is excluded and denied representation on account of his race or color."

9. "We believe that any law especially directed against the Negro to his detriment and singling him out because of his race or color is unfair and immoral, and should not be respected."

10. "We believe all men entitled to common human respect, and that our race should in no way tolerate any insults that may be interpreted to mean disrespect to our color."

11. "We deprecate the use of the term 'nigger' as applied to Negroes, and demand that the word 'Negro' be written with a capital 'N'."

Drafted and Adopted at Convention Held in New York, 1920, Over Which Hon. Marcus Garvey Presided as Chairman, and at Which He Was Elected Provisional President of Africa

12. "We believe that the Negro should adopt every means to protect himself against barbarous practices inflicted upon him because of color."

13. "We believe in the freedom of Africa for the Negro people of the world, and, by the principle of Europe for the Europeans and Asia for the Asiatics, we also demand Africa for the Africans at home and abroad."

14. "We believe in the inherent right of the Negro to possess himself of Africa, and that his possession of same shall not be regarded as an infringement on any claim or purchase made by any race or nation."

15. "We strongly condemn the cupidity of those nations of the world who, by open aggression, or secret schemes, have seized the territories and inexhaustible natural wealth of Africa, and we place on record our most solemn declaration to reclaim the treasures and possession of the vast continent of our forefathers."

16. "We believe all men should live in peace one with the other, but when races and nations provoke the ire of other races and nations by attempting to infringe upon their rights, war becomes inevitable, and the attempt in any way to free one's self or protect one's rights or heritage becomes justifiable."

17. "Whereas, The lynching, by burning, hanging, or any other means, of human beings is a barbarous practice, and a shame and disgrace to civilization, we therefore declare any country guilty of such atrocities outside the pale of civilization."

18. "We protest against the atrocious crime of whipping, flogging and overworking of the native tribes of Africa and Negroes everywhere. These are methods that should be abolished, and all means should be taken to prevent a continuance of such brutal practices."

19. "We protest against the atrocious practice of shaving the heads of Africans, especially of African women or individuals of Negro blood, when placed in prison as a punishment for crime by an alien race."

20. "We protest against segregated districts, separate public conveyances, industrial discrimination, lynchings and limitations of political privileges of any Negro citizen in any part of the world on account of race, color or creed, and will exert our full influence and power against all such."

21. "We protest against any punishment inflicted upon a Negro with severity, as against lighter punishment inflicted upon another of an alien race for like offense, as an act of prejudice and injustice, and should be resented by the entire race."

22. "We protest against the system of education in any country where Negroes are denied the same privileges and advantages as other races."

23. "We declare it inhuman and unfair to boycott Negroes from industries and labor in any part of the world."

24. "We believe in the doctrine of the freedom of the press, and we therefore emphatically protest against the suppression of Negro newspapers and periodicals in various parts of the world, and call upon Negroes everywhere to employ all available means to prevent such suppression."

25. "We further demand free speech universally for all men."

26. "We hereby protest against the publication of scandalous and inflammatory articles by an alien press tending to create racial strife and the exhibition of picture films showing the Negro as a cannibal."

27. "We believe in the self-determination of all peoples."

28. "We declare for the freedom of religious worship."

29. "With the help of Almighty God, we declare ourselves the sworn protectors of the honor and virtue of our women and children, and pledge our lives for their protection and defense everywhere, and under all circumstances from wrongs and outrages."

30. "We demand the right of unlimited and unprejudiced education for ourselves and our posterity forever."

31. "We declare that the teaching in any school by alien teachers to our boys and girls, that the alien race is superior to the Negro race, is an insult to the Negro people of the world."

32. "Where Negroes form a part of the citizenry of any country, and pass the civil service examination of such country, we declare them entitled to the same consideration as other citizens as to appointments in such civil service."

33. "We vigorously protest against the increasingly unfair and unjust treatment accorded Negro travelers on land and sea by the agents and employees of railroad and steamship companies and insist that for equal fare we receive equal privileges with travelers of other races."

34. "We declare it unjust for any country, State, or nation to enact laws tending to hinder and obstruct the free immigration of Negroes on account of their race and color."

35. "That the right of the Negro to travel unmolested throughout the world be not abridged by any person or persons, and all Negroes are called upon to give aid to a fellow-Negro when thus molested."

36. "We declare that all Negroes are entitled to the same right to travel over the world as other men."

37. "We hereby demand that the governments of the world recognize our leader and his representatives chosen by the race to look after the welfare of our people under such governments."

38. "We demand complete control of our social institutions without interference by any alien race or races."

39. "That the colors, Red, Black and Green, be the colors of the Negro race."

40. "Resolved, That the anthem, 'Ethiopia, Thou Land of Our Fathers,' etc., shall be the anthem of the Negro race."

A
Sense
of
Time...

3-7 million	Birthplace of humankind (Africa)
2 million	Stone tools, basic shelter (Tanzania, Africa)
1 million	Control and use of fire (South Africa)
250000	Emergence of Homo sapiens (modern man)
72000 – 58000	Projectile weapons, snares and traps (South Africa)
5000 – 3000	Early forms of writing e.g. Mande script (West Africa)
5000	Domestication of cattle (West Africa)
3400 - 650	Kingdoms of Egypt (Northeast Africa)
2620 - 2490	Pyramids of Giza is Constructed (Egypt, Africa)
2500 – 1500	Kerma Kingdom (Northeast Africa)
1500 – 500 CE	Nok Civilization (West Africa)
1070 – 350 CE	Kingdom of Kush (Northeast Africa)

ᴥᴥ Common Era (CE) ᴥᴥ

7	Arab Slave Trade Begins in East Africa
641	Arab invasion of Egypt, Africa
790 - 1235	Ghana Empire (West Africa)
800 – 1400	Great Wall of Benin is constructed (West Africa)
989	First university in the world (Timbuktu, West Africa)
1230 - 1600	Mali Empire (West Africa)
1526	First Transatlantic Slave Voyage (to Brazil)
1791 - 1804	Haitian Revolution
1816 - 1831	Major slave revolts in British West Indies
1831	Nat Turner's Slave Rebellion
1834	Abolition of slavery in Jamaica
1846 – 1928	Convict Lease System
1865	Abolition of slavery in the U.S.
1863 - 1877	Reconstruction Era
1877	Jim Crow laws begin
1885 - 1914	Colonization of Africa by Europe

☆ 1887	MARCUS GARVEY IS BORN
☆ 1914	Universal Negro Improvement Association is formed
1917	Espionage Act
1918	Sedition Act
☆ 1918 - 1933	Negro World Newspaper
☆ 1919	Est. Black Star Line, Liberty Halls, Negro Factories
☆ 1920	U.N.I.A. First Convention, New York
1921	Tulsa Riots
☆ 1923	Marcus Garvey is incarcerated
1934	Practice of "redlining" begins
☆ 1940	Marcus Garvey dies
1954 - 1968	Civil Rights Era
1956 – 1971	COINTELPRO (FBI Counterintelligence Program)
1964	Civil Rights Act
1965	Voting Rights Act
1966 - 1975	Black Power Movement
1971- present	Dramatic Rise in Incarceration Rates of Blacks in U.S

"Look for me in the whirlwind or the storm, look for me all around you, for, with God's grace, I shall come and bring with me countless millions of black slaves who have died in America and the West Indies and the millions in Africa to aid you in the fight for Liberty, Freedom and Life."
- Marcus Garvey

Made in the USA
Middletown, DE
03 January 2023

21279152R00027